LET'S FIND OUT ABOUT

Buddhist Temples

Anne Geldart

www.raintreepublishers.co.uk
Visit our website to find out more information about Raintree books.

To order:
☎ Phone 44 (0) 1865 888112
▤ Send a fax to 44 (0) 1865 314091
▣ Visit the Raintree Bookshop at www.raintreepublishers.co.uk to browse our catalogue and order online.

First published in Great Britain by Raintree, Halley Court, Jordan Hill, Oxford, OX2 8EJ, part of Harcourt Education.
Raintree is a registered trademark of Harcourt Education Ltd.

Editorial: Daniel Nunn and Sarah Chappelow
Design: Ron Kamen and Philippa Baile
Picture research: Hannah Taylor and Sally Claxton
Production: Duncan Gilbert
Religious consultant: Anil Goonewardene, The Buddhist Society, London

Originated by Modern Age
Printed in China
  by WKT Company Limited

ISBN 1 844 21141 X
10 09 08 07 06
10 9 8 7 6 5 4 3 2 1

British Library Cataloguing in Publication Data
Geldart, Anne
  Let's find out about Buddhist temples
  1. Temples, Buddhist – Juvenile literature
  2. Buddhism – Customs and practices – Juvenile literature
  I. Title II. Buddhist temples
  294.3'465
A full catalogue record for this book is available from the British Library.

Acknowledgements
The publishers would like to thank the following for permission to reproduce photographs:

Alamy Images p. **20** (World Religions Photo Library); Art Directors pp. **7** (Helene Rogers), **26** (Juliet Highet); Christine Osborne p. **15 top**; Corbis Royalty Free pp. **5**, **6**; Corbis pp. **8 top** (Craig Lovell), **13** (Jeremy Horner), **14** (Reuters), **15 bottom** (Chris Lisle), **16** (Kevin R. Morris), **24** (Michael Freeman), **25** (China Span LLC); Getty Images p. **8 bottom** (Photodisc); Trip pp. **4 top** (C. Rennie), **4 bottom** (H. Rogers), **9** (Richard Hammerton), **10** (T. Bognar), **11** (Peter Treanor), **12** (J. Sweeney), **17** (Dinodia), **18** (Francoise Pirson), **19** (Peter Treanor), **21** (B. Swanson), **22** (F. Good), **23** (H. Rogers), **27** (H. Rogers).

Cover photograph of Wat Benchamabophit, Bangkok, Thailand, reproduced with permission of Corbis/Kevin R. Morris.

The author would like to thank The Buddhist Society, Sally Masheder of the Network of Buddhist Organizations, and Clear Vision for their help.

Every effort has been made to contact copyright holders of any material reproduced in this book. Any omissions will be rectified in subsequent printings if notice is given to the publishers.

The paper used to print this book comes from sustainable resources.

Contents

Words appearing in the text in bold, like this, are explained in the Glossary. The Buddhist words used in this book are listed with a pronunciation guide on page 29.

What is a Buddhist temple?

A temple is a place where Buddhists meet to learn about the **Buddha**, and to talk about his teaching. Another name for a Buddhist temple is a **vihara**.

Some temples have beautiful gardens. These help people to feel peaceful and to think deeply about Buddhism. This is called **meditating**. Buddhists also meditate inside temples.

The Golden Temple in Kyoto, Japan, is very beautiful.

Buddhist temples are also called wats. This wat is in London, in the United Kingdom.

In countries where there are not many Buddhists, there may not be many specially built temples. Instead, Buddhists may set up **shrine** rooms inside other buildings. These can be rooms in a church or school, or even in a private home.

A Buddhist view

I go to a Buddhist temple to learn about the Buddha. We have stories that teach us how to live a good life. When I am older, I will learn how to meditate.
Andy, age eight, from Los Angeles, in the United States

Another kind of temple is a **pagoda**. Pagodas often have five floors. From bottom to top, these stand for earth, water, fire, wind, and space.

5

Buddhists and Buddhism

Buddhists are people who follow the teachings of the **Buddha**. The Buddha was born more than 2,000 years ago. His name was Prince Siddhartha Gautama.

When he was a young man, Siddhartha went out into the city. He saw people who were poor, sick, or dying. This made him very unhappy, so he decided to give up living like a prince. One night, six years later, he sat down to **meditate** under a **bodhi tree**.

This statue shows the Buddha teaching long ago.

Did you know

The Buddha was not a god or a **prophet**. He was a man who found a way of learning wisdom, kindness, and freedom from suffering.

Many thoughts came to him. The last was that you can only have true happiness (called "nirvana") when all greed, hatred, and **ignorance** are "blown out" like a candle. This idea became known as his **Enlightenment**. From that moment on, Prince Siddhartha Gautama became known as a "Buddha". This means "someone who has woken up".

The Buddha started to teach people about his ideas. His followers became the first Buddhists. Today there are Buddhists all over the world.

This monk is showering some young Buddhists with holy water.

Stupas, monasteries, and rupas

There are many different kinds of Buddhist temples, or **viharas**. **Stupas** are dome-shaped buildings that look like bells. They contain **relics** of important Buddhist teachers. Some stupas are very beautiful, like the gold stupa at Shwedagon **Pagoda** in Myanmar.

Monasteries are like schools for **monks**. Many Buddhists spend time in one. There is no special design for a monastery.

The gold stupa in Myanmar is a very large building.

Tengpoche Monastery is in the mountains of Nepal.

Inside the monastery there are rooms for study and **meditation**. There are also places for the monks to sleep. Very large monasteries may have separate temples or pagodas in the grounds.

A Buddhist **rupa** is an image or statue of the **Buddha**. It may show him standing, sitting, or lying down. There are always rupas inside temples.

This giant rupa stands by the roadside in Sri Lanka.

Inside a temple

The most important part of a temple is the **shrine** room. At the heart of the shrine, there is a **rupa**, or statue, of the **Buddha**. There may also be a tiny **stupa** next to the statue. This may have **relics** of a famous Buddhist teacher inside it.

Buddhists may bring gifts to the shrine room. These may be flowers, candles, and sticks of **incense**. Buddhists leave flowers to show their respect for the Buddha. They light candles as a sign of wisdom. Incense sticks are burned as a sign of truth.

This photo shows the shrine room inside a Buddhist temple in Myanmar.

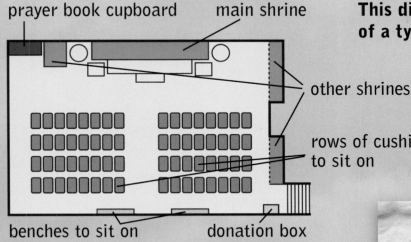

prayer book cupboard   main shrine

other shrines

rows of cushions
to sit on

benches to sit on   donation box

**This diagram shows the layout
of a typical shrine room.**

**These monks
are receiving
food from
visitors to a
temple.**

As well as decorations, there may
be a donation box where people
leave money to help pay for the
running of the temple. **Monks**
have no money of their own.

Did you know?

Not all shrines or
stupas are inside
temples. There are also
some small shrines at
the side of the road
or in the countryside.

Two of the most important Buddhist **shrines** are at Bodhgaya and Sarnath in India. They were both built in places where important things happened during the **Buddha's** lifetime.

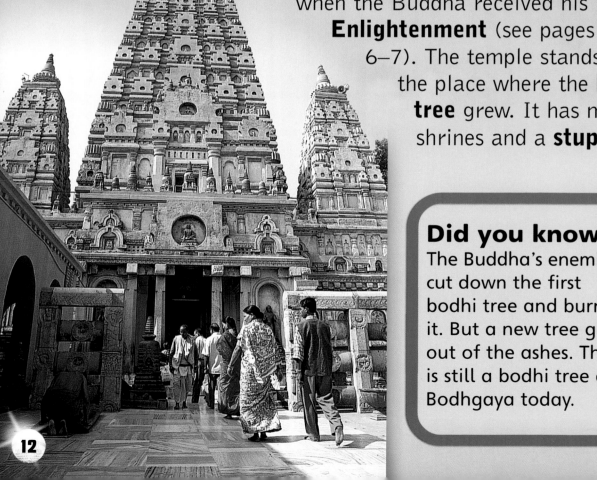

Buddhists visit the temple at Bodhgaya in India.

Every year, thousands of Buddhists visit Bodhgaya to celebrate the day when the Buddha received his **Enlightenment** (see pages 6–7). The temple stands on the place where the **bodhi tree** grew. It has many shrines and a **stupa**.

Did you know ?

The Buddha's enemies cut down the first bodhi tree and burnt it. But a new tree grew out of the ashes. There is still a bodhi tree at Bodhgaya today.

The brick stupa at Sarnath (which used to be called Isipatana) is built on the site of a deer park. This is where the Buddha taught his first followers. Today there are more than 300 million Buddhists in the world.

A monk sits by the stupa at Sarnath deer park.

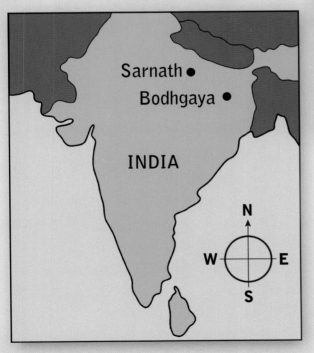

This map shows the locations of Sarnath and Bodhgaya in modern India.

Many Buddhist **monasteries** and temples are run by **monks**. Monks look after the monastery or temple and care for the **shrine**. They spend time studying the teachings of the **Buddha**.

A monk's life is often hard. Monks have only a short time to sleep, and eat only one meal a day. They shave all the hair from their head and faces and wear a simple, coloured robe.

In Thailand, children can start training to be monks at about the age of ten.

A Buddhist view

When I left primary school I became a monk. This is so that I can have a good education.

Anil, age ten, from Thailand

14

Monks are always men, but women can become **nuns**. They also shave their heads and follow the same rules as monks.

Monks spend as much time **meditating** as they can.

In most temples, a person who is not a monk may work there as a **volunteer**. In large monasteries, there may be a very senior monk in charge of lots of other monks.

What do people do at a Buddhist temple?

Most Buddhists go to a temple's **shrine** room to show respect for the **Buddha's** teachings. This is called **puja**. First they light candles as a sign of wisdom. Then they place gifts in front of the statue of the Buddha. These may be flowers, **incense**, rice, fruit, or water.

Puja also includes bowing down to the Buddha. Then people quietly think about their own behaviour. Finally, Buddhists **meditate** on how to become better people and be more helpful and kind to others.

Buddhists light candles at a temple in Thailand.

This man is turning prayer wheels outside a temple in Nepal.

In some Buddhist countries, there are prayer wheels outside temples. People turn them and this sends out the prayers written inside. In other places, small flags or pieces of paper may be attached to trees outside the temple. These hold messages or words from a short prayer.

Did you know

Many Buddhists do not think of puja as worship or prayer. This is because the Buddha is not a god and does not teach about a god.

Festivals

These children are cleaning an image of the Buddha in preparation for Vesak.

Buddhists often celebrate special days in their temples. For example, Buddhists believe that the **Buddha** was born, received **Enlightenment**, and died on the same day in different years. In some Buddhist countries, Buddhists celebrate all three events on the same day: the time of the full moon in May. This is called Vesak, or Buddha Day.

All images of the Buddha are washed and cleaned ready for the festival. On the day itself, Buddhists bring candles and **incense** to the temple. If there is a **stupa**, they walk around it three times to show their respect. Vesak is a happy time for Buddhists.

In other Buddhist countries, such as Japan, people celebrate the Buddha's birthday as a flower festival in April. This is called Hanamatsuri. People take flowers to the **shrines** and decorate statues of the Buddha that show him as a little child. In the street there is dancing, and there are food stalls for everyone to enjoy.

Buddhists decorate shrines with flowers on Hanamatsuri.

19

Family celebrations

Temples play an important role in many family celebrations. One important family ceremony is a funeral. Most Buddhists are cremated (burned to ash) after they die. A **monk** usually gathers up the ashes of the dead person. Then he buries the ashes at a cemetery. After the funeral, friends and neighbours celebrate the life of the dead person.

These Buddhists are carrying a coffin to be cremated at a funeral in Myanmar.

Having a baby is a happier event. Buddhist parents often take a new baby to a special ceremony at the temple. The monks there help the parents to choose a Buddhist name. They sprinkle water on the baby and say a **blessing**. Then they light a white candle and let the melted wax fall into a bowl of water. This shows the coming together of earth, air, fire, and water.

Buddhist weddings are led by a member of the family, such as a grandfather. Monks chant prayers or read from Buddhist teachings. After the wedding, there is usually a party.

This Buddhist couple in Sri Lanka is getting married. Their hands are being tied together with holy thread.

Being in a temple

Buddhist temples are special places, so people must always behave respectfully. Before going into a temple, they should take off their shoes and put them in the little wooden racks in the entrance hall. They should also make sure they are dressed sensibly. This might mean not wearing shorts or a short skirt, and making sure that all clothes are neat and clean.

Buddhists take off their shoes at a shrine in India.

Visitors should walk around quietly and respect the space of those who are **meditating**. There should be no running around or loud talk.

Every now and then, a bell will ring. Suddenly everything goes quiet. There will also be the sound of **monks** chanting Buddhist verses. This is part of **puja** – showing respect for the teachings of the **Buddha**.

A non-Buddhist view

When we visited a temple in Japan, we saw Buddhists coming and going in the temple all the time. They don't just come for worship. Lots of people just kneel or sit and think, for a few minutes.
Melanie, age eleven, from Cardiff in the United Kingdom

These Buddhists are meditating quietly at a temple in the United Kingdom.

A place to meet

Temples are places where Buddhists can learn more about their religion.

To most Buddhists, the temple is the centre of the **community**. Everyone goes at least once a week. They meet up with friends and talk about their lives. They may spend a short time in prayer or **meditation**.

Most temples offer classes in Buddhism. There may also be classes in fine handwriting and poetry, as well as other arts and crafts.

Many different groups may meet at the temple. For example, the **Buddha** said his followers should avoid killing anything. Buddhists meet to talk about how they should care for wildlife.

Other groups try to bring hope and healing to people who are poor or sick. This is because Buddhism teaches that people must not be greedy while other people are hungry.

Monks practise kung fu at a monastery in China.

Did you know
Some temples hold classes in **martial arts**, such as kendo, ju-jitsu, and kung fu. In Japan, children learn these sports in school.

Devotion at home

This family is doing yoga together.

Buddhism is a religion for every day. This means that Buddhists always try to make time for **devotion**, **meditation**, and study at home.

Some Buddhists do yoga as part of their religion. This is a set of exercises that helps people to calm their minds. In China and Japan, families often do tai chi – a special routine that is like meditation with actions. Buddhists may do these exercises at home, at school, or at work.

Most Buddhist homes have a **shrine**. The shrine room is always the best room in the house, and anyone entering the room must take off their shoes and socks.

A Buddhist view

Every home in our town has a shrine room. My parents had to wait seven years for their big shrine to come. Until then, we just had a small, wooden one.

Kotaro, age eleven, from Japan

A shrine in a Buddhist home is often just a small statue of the **Buddha**, a candle holder, an **incense** holder, flowers, and some small dishes for gifts.

Buddhism around the world

Buddhism began in India, thousands of years ago. It spread from India to Sri Lanka, and then to Myanmar, Thailand, and other countries in South-East Asia. Its teachers also took it north to the kingdoms in the great Himalayan mountains. Then it found its way into China, Korea, and Japan.

Today there are more than 300 million Buddhists worldwide. There are also many Buddhists in the West. Some are Buddhists from Asian countries who have moved there. Others are people who have converted to Buddhism.

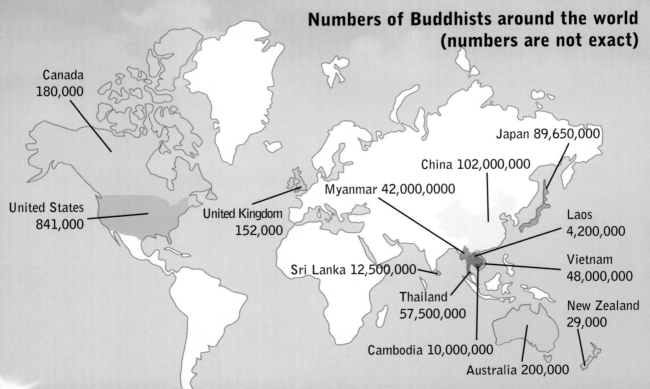

Numbers of Buddhists around the world (numbers are not exact)

Canada 180,000

Japan 89,650,000

China 102,000,000

Myanmar 42,000,0000

United States 841,000

United Kingdom 152,000

Laos 4,200,000

Vietnam 48,000,000

Sri Lanka 12,500,000

Thailand 57,500,000

New Zealand 29,000

Cambodia 10,000,000

Australia 200,000

Buddhist words

These are the Buddhist words that have been used in this book. You can find out how to say them by reading the pronunciation guide in the brackets after each word.

bodhi [bo-di] – a type of tree. The Buddha sat under a bodhi tree on the night he received Enlightenment.

Buddha [bud-da] – someone who has received Enlightenment. The Buddha was born in India as a prince more than 2,000 years ago.

Hanamatsuri [ha-na mat-soo-ri] – a celebration of the Buddha's birthday, held in April

ju-jitsu [joo-jit-soo] – a Japanese form of unarmed self-defence

kendo [ken-doh] – a traditional Japanese form of fencing, using wooden swords

kung fu [kung foo] – a Chinese form of unarmed fighting similar to ju-jitsu

nirvana [ner-vah-nah] – a state where a Buddhist has finally lost all sense of suffering and is "at one" with the universe

pagoda [pa-go-dah] – a Buddhist building with five floors, usually beautifully decorated

puja [poo-jah] – acts of worship at home or in the temple

rupa [roo-pah] – a statue or image. Rupas of the Buddha can be seated, lying down, or standing.

Siddhartha Gautama [sid-art-ah gwa-ta-ma] – the person who became the Buddha

stupa [stoo-pah] – a bell-shaped building containing relics (such as bones) of a famous teacher of Buddhism

tai chi [tie-chee] – exercises that help to calm the mind

Vesak [wey-sack] – the celebration of the Buddha's birth, Enlightenment, and death – also called "Buddha Day"

vihara [vee-ha-rah] – another name for a temple

wat [wot] – another name for a temple

yoga [yo-gah] – the practice of self-control and balance as an aid to meditation

Glossary

blessing wish for good things and happiness for a person

bodhi tree tree under which the Buddha received Enlightenment

Buddha someone who has received Enlightenment. The Buddha was born in India as a prince more than 2,000 years ago.

community group of people who have something in common

devotion respect, love, and loyalty to someone or something

Enlightenment when the Buddha became aware of the truth

ignorance not knowing about something

incense substance that gives off a nice smell when burned

martial arts kinds of fighting developed in Japan, China, and Tibet

meditate spend time being quiet and thinking about something very deeply, for religious reasons

monastery place where monks live away from other people, and study and practise their religion

monk man who gives up ordinary life to live for his religion

nun woman who gives up ordinary life to live for her religion

pagoda Buddhist building with five roofs

prophet someone sent by God with messages for people

puja acts of devotion at home or in the temple

relic religious object from the past, often some part or reminder of a holy person

rupa statue or image

shrine a very holy place

stupa bell-shaped building containing relics (such as bones) of a famous teacher of Buddhism

vihara another name for a Buddhist temple

volunteer person who works without being paid

Finding out more

Visiting a Buddhist temple

Buddhists welcome visitors to their temples. Many people enjoy spending time in temples. They may be interested in finding out the history of the temple and the Buddhist religion. They may feel that the temple is a special place where they can sit quietly and think about things.

When people visit a temple, they should always behave respectfully. They should remove their shoes before going inside. Normally, they should not make too much noise or rush around. If people see someone meditating, it is especially important not to be noisy. People who visit a temple should always leave things as they find them.

More books to read

Celebrations!: Wesak, Anita Ganeri (Heinemann Library, 2001)

Holy Places: Bodh Gaya, Mandy Ross (Heinemann Library, 2002)

Religions of the World: Buddhism, Sue Penney (Heinemann Library, 2002)

Useful websites

http://www.uri.org/kids/world_budd.htm
This website about Buddhism has been specially written for young readers.

http://www.bbc.co.uk/religion/religions/buddhism/index.shtml
This website from the BBC looks at all aspects of Buddhism.

Index

Titles in the *Let's Find Out About* series include:

Hardback   1-844-21141-X

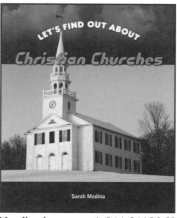

Hardback   1-844-21138-X

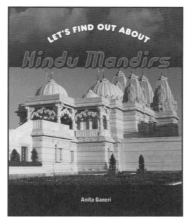

Hardback   1-844-21140-1

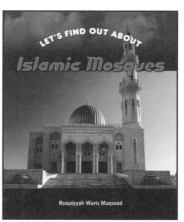

Hardback   1-844-21142-8

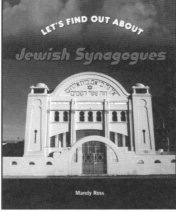

Hardback   1-844-21139-8

Hardback   1-844-21143-6

Find out about other titles from Raintree on our website www.raintreepublishers.co.uk